LET'S LEARN ABOUT...

THE LAND

PROJECT BOOK

CBEEBIES

K2

 Pearson

Pearson Education Limited
KAO Two, KAO Park, Harlow, Essex, CM17 9NA, England
and Associated Companies around the world

First published 2020

ISBN: 978-1-292-33457-8

Set in Mundo Sans

Printed in China SWTC/01

Acknowledgements
The publishers and author(s) would like to thank the following people and institutions for their feedback and
comments during the development of the material: Marcos Mendonça, Leandra Dias, Viviane Kirmeliene, Rhiannon
Ball, Simara H. Dal'Alba, Mônica Bicalho and GB Editorial.

The publishers would also like to thank all the teachers who contributed to the development of *Let's learn about...*:
Adriano de Paula Souza, Aline Ramos Teixeira Santo, Aline Vitor Rodrigues Pina Pereira, Ana Paula Gomez Montero,
Anna Flávia Feitosa Passos
Camila Jarola, Celiane Junker Silva, Edegar França Junior, Fabiana Reis Yoshio, Fernanda de Souza Thomaz, Luana da
Silva, Michael Iacovino Luidvinavicius, Munique Dias de Melo
Priscila Rossatti Duval Ferreira Neves, Sandra Ferito, and schools that took part in Construindo Juntos.

Author Acknowledgements
Rhiannon S. Ball

Image Credit(s):
BBC Worldwide Learning: 5, 7, 7, 9, 11, 13, 13, 17, 19, 21, 23, 25, 27, 29, 31, 33, 35
Pearson Education Ltd: Silva Serviços de Educação 5, 5, 5, 5, 5, 7, 11, 13, 15, 17, 17, 17, 19, 21, 23, 25, 27, 29, 29, 31, 31,
33, 35, 35, 35, 35, 49, 49, 49, 49, 49, 49, 51, 51
Shutterstock.com: BeRad 7, Iryna Dobrovynska 17, Natalia Sheinkin 9, NotionPic 35

Illustration Acknowledgements
Illustrated by Filipe Laurentino and Silva Serviços de Educação.

Cover illustration © Filipe Laurentino

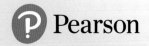

CONTENTS

LOOK, THINK, AND DRAW.

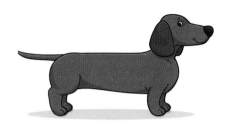  

LOOK, THINK, AND DRAW.

LOOK, THINK, AND DRAW.

LOOK, FIND, AND STICK.

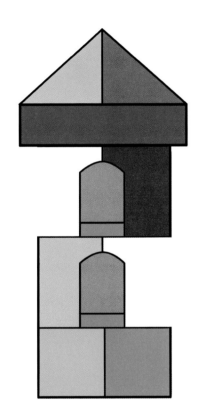

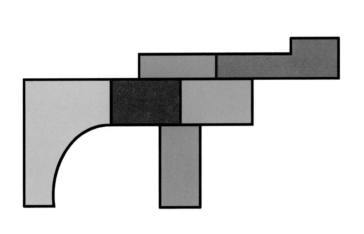

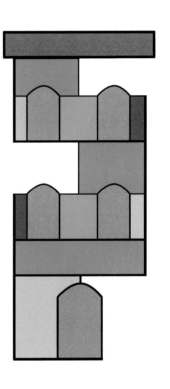

LOOK, THINK, AND STICK.

LOOK, THINK, AND DRAW.

LOOK, THINK, AND MATCH.

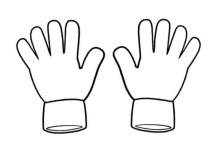

LOOK, THINK, AND DRAW.

LOOK, THINK, DRAW, AND COLOR.

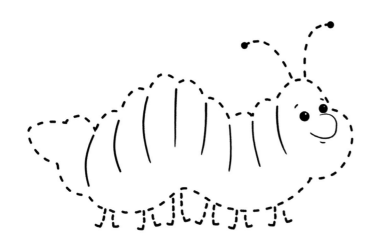

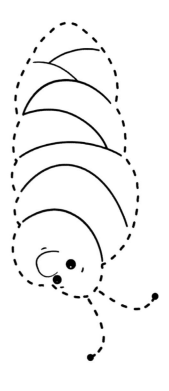

LOOK, FIND, AND STICK.

LOOK, THINK, AND DRAW.

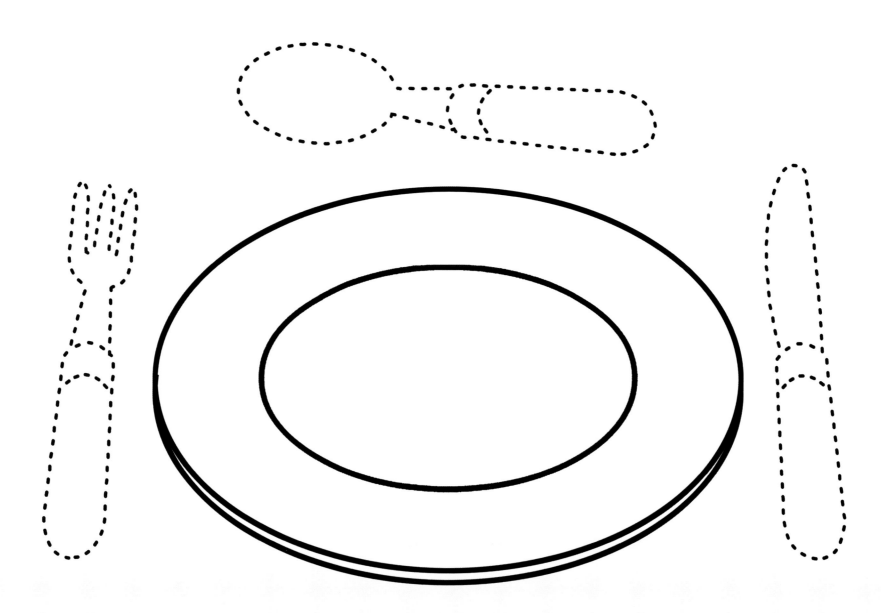

LOOK, COLOR, AND DRAW.

LOOK AND THINK. MATCH AND COLOR.

LOOK, DRAW, AND MATCH.

LOOK AND STICK. COLOR.

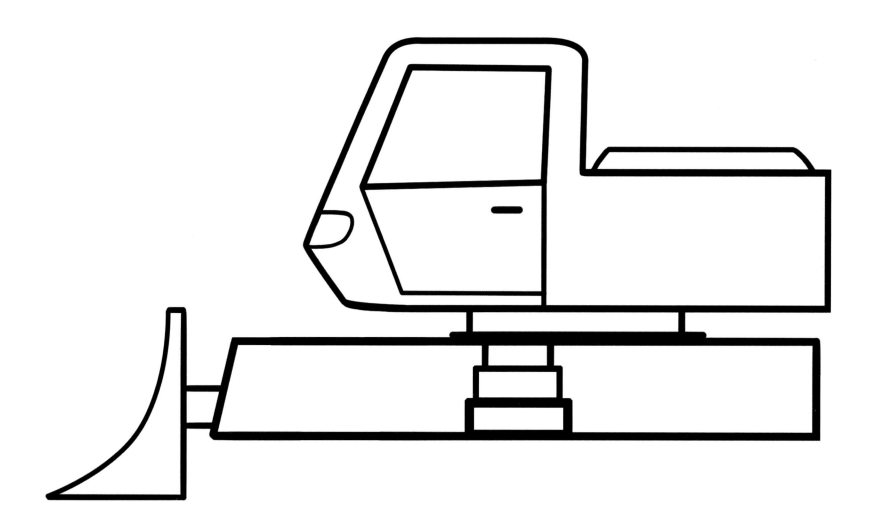

LOOK, THINK, AND DRAW.

DRAWING

DRAW.

DRAW.

DRAW.

DRAW.

STICKERS